TESTOSTERONE AND MUSCLE: RECIPES TO GET YOU LEAN AND FIT

By

JACKSON STEELE

TABLE OF CONTENTS

INTRODUCTION

What Is Bodybuilding Diets

Bodybuilding diets are designed to build muscle and reduce body fat, in combination with strengthening exercise programs. There are many variants of this diet, but they all focus on foods rich in protein and complex carbohydrates, such as pasta, cereals, and whole wheat bread. Normally, on a bodybuilding diet you gain weight.

What Benefits Does It Bring?

- Increased strength and muscle mass
- Increased metabolism
- Improved health and physical appearance

What Risks Does It Pose And What Precautions Should Be Taken?

Bodybuilding diets often place more importance on physical appearance than health. Major dietary changes must be made little by little to allow the body to adapt; for example, a sharp reduction or increase in calories can cause the body to store lipids. Many bodybuilding diets emphasize nutrient supplementation. Excessive protein intake, as can occur with supplemental protein powders, can cause serious health problems such as dehydration and kidney damage. People with heart disease or other health problems should consult their doctor before starting a bodybuilding diet and exercise program.

Bodybuilding diets are not recommended for pregnant and lactating women. Bodybuilding diets and exercise routines vary greatly and can be confusing. Anyone with arthritis, back problems, or joint problems should consult their doctor before starting any physical exercise program.

How Does It Work?

Bodybuilding diets typically require 2,500 to 5,500 calories per day for men and 1,500 to 3,000 for women, depending on the type and level of exercise. Every 0.45 kg of muscle burns up to 50 calories a day, so adding 4.5 kg of muscle can burn up to 500 more calories.

The suggested proportions of carbohydrates, proteins and fats vary considerably. Some diets require 50% to 60% of calories from carbohydrates. The complex carbohydrates found in whole grain cereals, pasta and bread, beans, and most vegetables are eaten throughout the day. Simple carbohydrates, composed of one or two sugars and present in fruit and sugary foods, are taken immediately after doing the exercise table to accelerate muscle restoration, recovery and repair.

Protein builds muscle mass, helps protect muscle tissue, and helps improve recovery after vigorous exercise with weights. However, not all protein that is ingested goes directly to the muscles. In most bodybuilding diets, 0.45 g to 0.68 g of protein is recommended daily per pound of lean body mass (body weight minus body fat). Monounsaturated and polyunsaturated fats are healthy fats that make up an important part of bodybuilding diets for muscle building and overall health.

These fats are found in avocado, most nuts, fatty fish, flax, extra virgin olive oil, and rapeseed oil. In most bodybuilding diets, it is recommended to eat 6 to 8 small meals a day, starting with breakfast. The meal before the exercise table should be rich in carbohydrates to increase physical performance and improve muscle recovery. In many bodybuilding diets, it is recommended to have a meal after the exercise table that has twice the calories, protein and carbohydrates of the other meals.

Drinking at least 2 liters of water a day, with about 60 ml every 15 minutes during exercise, helps control appetite. Cold water increases metabolism. Most bodybuilding diets require supplemental nutrient intakes including protein powders, as well as weight training and cardio 3-7 days a week.

What Is The Purpose Of Dieting In Bodybuilding?

Bodybuilding diets are a proven tool for athletes looking to build musclewant to reduce their body fat. Especially in competitions, with the right diet, you increase your chances of winning before the decisive day. With an effective bodybuilding diet plan, men can reduce their body fat percentage down to 10%. Women who naturally have more body fat, on the other hand, make it to 12%. One also speaks of defining the muscles. They should be clearly visible under the skin. But a bodybuilding diet doesn't work in a few days. Many athletes start to prepare for the big day with the right nutrition 16 weeks before the competition. The bodybuilding diet plan is constantly adapted to the current body condition. If the first measures are unsuccessful, the protein rations, for example, mustand carbohydrates are reduced or increased. You can find out more about this in the following paragraphs.

Basic Requirements For A Bodybuilding Diet

How fast you burn fat depends on your metabolism. You can promote the process with physical activity, but for the most part it is genetically predisposed. Researchers distinguish between three different types of metabolism, which can be identified based on body structure. In order to know what to eat on a bodybuilding diet, it is important to know your very own body type. In the following we will introduce you to the three possible types.

The ectomorphic body type:

- Grown tall
- Slim stature
- Narrow shoulders
- Long limbs compared to the upper body
- Faster metabolism
- Low body fat percentage
- Hardly gains weight, no matter how much he eats
- Is one of the hard gainers
- Difficulty building muscle
- Not very resilient
- Takes a long time to regenerate

Training And Nutrition Tips:

The ectomorphic physique is both a blessing and a curse. On the one hand, you have hardly any problem areas and you can always eat your fill without worrying about gaining weight. However, your metabolism burns calories so quickly that you lack the basis for building muscle.

Extensive cardio training would result in an even higher calorie consumption. Instead, you should specifically target your muscles. Strength training with heavy weights and a few repetitions is perfect. After a strenuous workout, treat yourself to several days of rest so that your body can recover. Compared to the other body types, you need a little longer for regeneration.

You can eat as much as you like while eating. Fat pads will not become visible anytime soon. A mix of carbohydrates and high-quality proteins is ideal for absorbing energy and muscle building blocks.

The mesomorphic body type:

- Slender hips
- Broad shoulders
- Comparatively long upper body
- Typical V-shape in men
- Hourglass shape in women
- Builds muscle mass quickly
- Low body fat percentage
- Very athletic appearance
- Short regeneration
- Quickly breaks down love handles

Training and nutrition tips:

As a mesomorphic body type, you can consider yourself lucky. Your physique offers ideal conditions to quickly lose fat and build muscle. It is best to combine strength training with endurance sports in a balanced relationship. Above all, it is important that your training plan is varied.

The same applies to your nutrition plan. Both carbohydrates and proteins are allowed to a large extent. However, if you find that carbohydrates cause weight gain during your bodybuilding diet, you should reduce the ration and consume more protein.

The endomorphic body type:

- Stocky, rounded stature
- Short limbs
- Broad torso
- Wide hips
- Looks soft and not very muscular
- High body fat percentage
- Builds muscles quickly
- Short regeneration phase
- Slow metabolism
- Is increasing rapidly
- Great difficulties in the definition phase

Training and nutrition tips:

The endomorphic body type corresponds to the softgainer. Your high body fat percentage is on the one hand a hindrance when you want to show off your muscles, but at the same time it helps you to build muscle mass quickly. If you focus more on endurance training, you will be able to control your weight and prevent flab. With additional strength training, you will strengthen your muscles.

Unfortunately, as an endomorphic body type, you have to pay close attention to your food choices. Fat should make up the smallest part of your diet. Carbohydrates should also be chosen carefully. After training, however, they are essential to fill your glycogen stores. Proteins should be your main source of nutrients. They keep you full for a long time and make it even easier for you to build muscle.

What Do The Experts Think

Most bodybuilding diets are accepted as healthy and effective for increasing muscle mass and reducing fat. Although insufficient carbohydrate consumption can have negative effects on performance and duration of exercise, a high percentage of calories from carbohydrates is not necessarily effective either. Studies have shown that weightlifters need more protein for muscle maintenance, growth and repair, but protein intake should not exceed 1.5g - 2g per kilo. A protein intake of more than 1.4g - 1.8g per kilo or 15-20% of daily calories has no beneficial effect.

You will find more information in the American Academy of Nutrition and Dietetics articles on "Strengthening and Muscle Mass" and "Eating Right for Resistance Training."

8 Rules In Your Diet For Muscle Growth

➢ **Eat More Protein**

Proteins help your muscle rebuilding and growth. You 'tear' the muscle and the proteins rebuild it and give it volume. They provide the essential amino acids for muscle and stimulate the production of insulin and growth hormone. For example, someone who weighs about 75 kilos, should consume at least 170 grams of protein per day. That is, 250 grams of chicken, a cup of cottage cheese, a fillet of veal, two eggs and half a liter of milk, for example.

➢ **Consume More Calories**

If you do fitness to gain muscle you cannot eat as if your goal is to lose weight. To gain half a kilo of muscle you would need about 2,800 calories daily. With certain criteria, but the rule is basic: if you go to the gym, you have to eat a lot, especially if you are a beginner.

In fact, in some studies, researchers found that the lifters with the most muscle gains were the men who ate the most.

➢ **Eat Every 3 Hours**

White's plan calls for increasing her calories to 3,000 per day. That's a lot of food to eat in three parts, so he recommends eating every three hours or so, a total of six a day; It will also help you stay full with a constant supply of macronutrients and micronutrients. And at least 30 grams of protein per intake.

➢ **Bet On A Correct Combination Of Macros**

Yes, many proteins, but without neglecting carbohydrates and fats. Each person should find their correct combination of macros based on their daily physical activity. Many nutritionists and preparers recommend 50 percent carbohydrates, 25 percent protein, and 25 percent fat.

➢ **Stay Hydrated**

Exercise-induced dehydration slows down motor neurons, and that translates into: feeling more fatigued and decreasing your performance. In addition, a study in the Journal of Applied Physiology concluded that dehydrated fitness athletes produced more cortisol, the stress hormone, while reducing the release of testosterone, the great ally for your muscles.

➢ Find Your Ideal Whey Protein

For after your workout, drink your whey protein shake, which will provide you with about 25 grams of protein per serving. It is digested very quickly, nourishes the muscles earlier and has a high concentration of branched-chain amino acids, essential for protein synthesis.

➢ Have A Banana Before Your Workout

Why? Because banana is rich in electrolytes, which help to contract muscles and exercise depletes electrolytes quickly. You will avoid cramps. As an alternative to banana, a Greek yogurt or low sugar sports drink.

➢ Schedule Your Meals

If you are serious about gaining more muscle, be serious about being more disciplined when you eat. You can start by creating a meal plan and sticking to strict schedules. Eat breakfast shortly after you wake up and stop eating three hours before you go to bed. Remember, your body repairs and builds muscles while you sleep. Eating right before bed can interrupt your sleep and affect your rest. Remember, muscle grows while you sleep too.

TURKISH SCRAMBLED EGGS – MENEMEN

Servings: 4

INGRIDIENT

- 3 tomatoes
- 3 hot peppers
- 150 g Turkish garlic sausage
- 2 small onions
- 3 tbsp butter
- salt
- pepper
- 8 eggs
- 150 g feta

PREPARATION

Wash and quarter the tomatoes and remove the core. Cut the tomatoes into small cubes. Wash and core the peppers and cut into fine rings. Cut the sausage into pieces. Peel the onions and cut them into rings.

Heat 2 tbsp butter in a pan and sauté the onions. Fry the sausage and pepperoni. Finally add the tomatoes and fry them briefly. Season with salt and pepper.

Whisk eggs, season. Heat the rest of the butter in a second pan, pour in the eggs. Let it set over low heat, stirring again and again. To serve, place the eggs and sausage vegetables in a bowl and crumble the feta over the hot egg.

Wash and quarter the tomatoes and remove the core. Cut the tomatoes into small cubes. Wash and core the peppers and cut into fine rings. Cut the sausage into pieces. Peel the onions and cut them into rings.

CLASSIC SCRAMBLED EGGS

Servings: 4

INGREDIENTS

- 8 eggs
- 1 teaspoon salt
- 3 tbsp milk
- 2 tbsp butter
- 1 sprig (s) of parsley

PREPARATION

Put the eggs, salt and milk in a bowl and whisk with a whisk.

Heat the butter in a non-stick pan over medium heat. Swivel the pan so that the butter is heated evenly in the pan.

Whip the egg mixture again and add to the pan. Let the eggs set for about 15 seconds and then stir or use a spatula to move the solid portions. Continue until the egg mixture is no longer liquid and has reached the desired cooking point. Garnish with fresh parsley if necessary.

QUICK PAPRIKA OMELETS

Servings: 2

INGREDIENT

- 1 red pepper
- 0.5 bunch of chives
- 6 eggs
- 6 tbsp milk
- 80 g grated Gouda cheese
- salt
- pepper
- 4 tbsp olive oil
- 80 g salad mix
- 4 tbsp ready-made balsamic dressing

PREPARATION

Clean and wash the peppers and cut into small cubes. Cut the chives into small rolls. In a bowl, whisk the eggs, milk, Gouda cheese and 4 tbsp chives together vigorously. Season with salt and pepper.

Heat 1 tablespoon of olive oil in a small pan, add half of the egg mixture to the pan. Let the eggs set on medium heat for 3-4 minutes. Place half of the Gouda cheese and half of the paprika on top and cover and cook for 2-3 minutes.

Fold the omelette halfway over and keep it warm in the hot oven at 100 degrees (convection not recommended). Process the remaining ingredients into a second omelette. Serve the omelets sprinkled with the remaining chives.

Put one omelette on each plate. Serve half of the salad and half of the dressing.

HERB QUARK

Servings: 8

INGREDIENTS

- 0.25 bunch of parsley
- 0.25 bunch of chives
- 1 small red onion
- 4 pieces of cherry tomatoes
- 1 spring onion
- 0.25 cucumber
- 500 g cream quark
- 1 tbsp olive oil
- salt
- pepper

* 1 organic lemon (zest and juice)

PREPARATION

Wash, pat dry and chop the parsley if necessary. Put a few leaves aside as decoration for later. Cut the chives diagonally into fine rings.

Peel the onion and cut into fine cubes. Wash and cut the cherry tomatoes into eighths. Cut off the roots of the spring onions, peel off the outer leaf and cut diagonally into rings.

Wash the cucumber, cut in half lengthways and scrape out the core with a spoon. Then grate the cucumber coarsely.

Put the quark together with lemon zest, lemon juice, olive oil, salt and pepper in a bowl and stir with a whisk until smooth. Add the prepared ingredients, mix everything and garnish with a few parsley leaves.

OVERNIGHT OATS WITH SKYR

Servings: 4

INGREDIENTS

- 1 cup
- 6 tablespoons of crispy oat flakes
- 1 tbsp almond sticks
- 1 teaspoon grated chocolate
- 100 ml milk
- 8 tbsp skyr
- 1 teaspoon honey
- 50 g blueberries

PREPARATION

6 tablespoons of crispy oat flakes 1 tbsp almond sticks 1 teaspoon grated chocolate 100 ml milk

Put 6 tablespoons of crispy oat flakes in a swing-top glass and mix with the almond sticks and grated chocolate. Then cover with milk and let stand in the refrigerator overnight.

Mix together the skyr and honey and pour over it. Wash the berries, drain them and place on the skyr.

Put in the fridge overnight and enjoy the next morning.

SMALL LOW-CARB BREAD

Servings: 4

INGREDIENTS

- 12 pieces
- 1 tbsp wheat flour
- 100 g ground almonds
- 50 g of crushed flaxseed
- 2 tbsp wheat bran
- 0.5 tsp salt
- 1 teaspoon baking powder
- 250 g low-fat quark
- 4 eggs
- 1 tbsp sunflower seeds

* 1 tbsp pumpkin seeds

PREPARATION

1 tbsp wheat flour 100g ground almonds 50g of crushed flaxseed 2 tbsp wheat bran 0.5 tsp salt 1 teaspoon baking powder 250g low-fat quark 4 eggs

Mix the flour with the almonds, flax seeds, wheat bran, salt and baking powder. Mix the low-fat quark and eggs in a bowl. Gradually fold in the flour mixture and work everything into a dough. Let rest for about 10 minutes.

Put the dough in the loaf pan (dimensions: 20 x 9 cm) and distribute the sunflower and pumpkin seeds evenly on top. Lightly press.

Bake the dough in a preheated oven at 180 ° C top / bottom heat for about 40 minutes. Take the bread out of the mold and let it cool on a wire rack.

LOW CARB PIZZA WITH BACON AND FRIED EGGS

Servings: 2

INGREDIENTS

- 2 servings
- 1 fresh lizza batter
- 50 g brie
- 2 tbsp green pesto
- 2 tbsp bacon cubes
- 2 eggs
- Salt
- Pepper
- 2 stalk (s) of fresh basil

PREPARATION

Preheat the oven to 200 degrees circulating air. Place the Lizza dough on a baking sheet lined with baking paper and prick several times with a fork. Pre-bake in a hot oven for 5 minutes, then remove from the oven.

Dice the brie. Spread the pesto on the lizza dough, spread the brie and bacon cubes on top. Put it back in the oven for 2-3 minutes so that the cheese runs smoothly.

Beat the eggs and let them slide carefully onto the lizza. Bake in the oven for another 7 minutes, until the eggs are cooked to the desired level.

Take out of the oven, season with salt and pepper and garnish with the fresh basil leaves.

HERBAL OMELETTE

Servings: 4

INGREDIENT

- 1 red onion
- 1 handful of chervil
- 0.5 bunch of chives
- 1 bed (s) of cress
- 8 REWE organic eggs
- salt
- pepper
- 8 EL sprudeliges mineral water
- 2 tbsp REWE organic sunflower oil

PREPARATION

Peel onion and chop finely. Wash the chervil, shake dry and chop finely. Wash the chives and cut into rolls. Cut the cress from the bed, wash and shake dry.

Whisk the eggs with salt, pepper and mineral water for about 15 seconds. Stir in the chervil and chives.

Heat 1 tablespoon of oil in a pan, sweat half of the onion cubes, then add half of the egg mixture. Let it set over low heat, after about 5 minutes turn the herb omelette and let it set for another 2 minutes. Bake the second omelette in the same way. Cut into pieces of cake and sprinkle with cress on top.

SCRAMBLED TOFU - VEGAN SCRAMBLED EGGS

Servings: 4

INGREDIENTS

- 400 g plain tofu
- 1 onion
- 4 tbsp sunflower oil
- 0.5 tsp turmeric
- pepper
- 1 pinch (s) of paprika powder
- salt
- 8 tbsp unsweetened soy yogurt
- 1 teaspoon kala namak
- 0.25 bunch of chives

- 4 slice (s) of farmhouse bread

PREPARATION

First cut the tofu into thin slices and then finely shred. Peel the onion and cut into fine cubes.

Heat oil in a pan. Fry the tofu and onion in it for about 5 minutes. Season with turmeric, pepper, paprika and salt.

Turn the stove down, stir in the soy yoghurt and fry for another 3 minutes. Finally, season with Kala Namak.

Wash the chives, shake dry and cut into fine rolls. Toasting or toasting bread. Serve the tofu egg on the bread and sprinkle with chives.

MUSHROOM AND AVOCADO OMELETTE

Servings: 4

INGREDIENTS

- 400 g of brown mushrooms
- 1 onion
- 2 tbsp olive oil
- salt
- pepper
- 10 eggs
- 3 tbsp milk
- 150 g fresh spinach
- 150 g feta cheese
- 1 avocado
- 2 tbsp quark

PREPARATION

Clean the mushrooms, cut into thin slices. Peel onions and cut them into fine pieces. Fry the mushrooms and onions in 1 tablespoon of oil. Season with salt and pepper, remove from the pan and set aside.

Whisk eggs with milk, season with salt and pepper. Bake 4 omelets one after the other from the egg mixture in a coated frying pan with the remaining oil.

Wash spinach, shake dry. Roughly crumble the feta. Cut the avocado into wedges.

Spread a thin layer of quark on each omelette. Fill half with mushrooms, spinach, avocado and feta. Fold up and serve.

SALMON SCRAMBLED EGG SANDWICH

Servings: 4

INGREDIENTS

- 8 rewe organic eggs
- 3 tbsp rewe organic low-fat milk
- salt
- pepper
- 2 tbsp rapeseed oil
- 10 g chives
- 4 slice (s) of whole meal bread
- 200 g rewe organic smoked salmon

PREPARATION

Whisk eggs with milk in a bowl. Season with salt and pepper. Slightly heat the rapeseed oil in the pan. Put the eggs in the pan, let them set for about 15 seconds and stir. Fry until you have reached the desired cooking point. Stir it again and again.

Wash the chives, cut into thin rolls and mix half with the scrambled eggs.

Cover the bread slices with scrambled eggs and smoked salmon. Garnish with chives.

PROTEIN BREAD SANDWICH WITH SMOKED TOFU, AVOCADO & SPROUTS

Servings: 4

INGREDIENTS

- 200 g smoked tofu
- 1 tbsp sunflower oil
- 8 slice (s) of PEMA protein bread, hearty
- 0.5 cucumber
- 1 tomato
- 1 lemon
- 2 avocados
- salt
- pepper

- 100 g sprouts (e.g. alfalfa sprouts)
- 2 tbsp vegan mayonnaise

PREPARATION

Cut the smoked tofu into 0.5 cm thick strips and fry them in a non-stick pan with oil until crispy brown. Put the tofu aside and briefly toast the protein bread on both sides in the pan.

Wash the cucumber and tomato, remove the stem of the tomato and cut both into fine slices. Halve the lemon and squeeze out the juice. Halve the avocados, remove the stone and remove the pulp from the skin.

Mix the avocado and lemon juice with a hand blender to a fine cream and season with salt and pepper.

Brush half of the bread slices with the avocado cream and top with smoked tofu, tomato, cucumber and sprouts. Spread the remaining bread slices thinly with vegan mayonnaise and use it to close the sandwich. Halve the sandwich diagonally.

OMELETTE WITH VEGETABLE AND FETA FILLING

Servings: 4

INGREDIENTS

- 2 Portionen
- 4 eggs
- 50 ml of milk
- pepper
- salt
- 100 g cherry tomatoes
- 1 zucchini
- 0.5 eggplant
- 1 clove (s) of garlic
- 50 g black olives

- 4 tbsp oil
- 2 stalk (s) basil
- 100 g feta

PREPARATION

Whisk eggs with milk, pepper and salt. Halve tomatoes. Cut the zucchini and aubergine into small cubes. Peel and press the garlic. Cut the olives into small pieces.

Heat 2 tablespoons of oil in a pan and fry the zucchini and aubergine with the garlic. Season with salt and pepper and sprinkle with basil. Fold in tomatoes and olives.

Heat the remaining oil in a pan and fry half of the egg mixture on both sides. Place on a plate and top with half of the vegetable mixture. Sprinkle with feta and close.

YOGURT BOWL WITH COCONUT CHIPS

Servings: 2

INGREDIENTS

- 100 g raspberries
- 100 g blueberries
- 500 g REWE organic yoghurt mild
- 4 tbsp oatmeal
- 70 g almonds
- 20 g coconut chips

PREPARATION

Wash the raspberries and blueberries and pat dry carefully.

Divide the yoghurt between 2 bowls.

Place a row of raspberries, oat flakes, blueberries and almonds on each bowl.
Finally sprinkle with coconut chips.

OMELETTE WITH CHANTERELLES

Servings: 4

INGREDIENTS

- 4 Portionen
- 350 g chanterelles
- 2 onions
- 1 bunch of chives
- 100 g mountain cheese
- 8 eggs
- 150 ml of cream
- salt
- pepper
- 2 tbsp oil

PREPARATION

Clean the chanterelles. Peel and finely chop the onions. Wash the chives, shake dry and cut into rolls. Rasp cheese.

Whisk eggs and cream together. Season with salt, pepper and chives.

Heat the oil in an ovenproof pan. Fry the chanterelles for about 5 minutes. Then add onions and cook for another 4 minutes. Season with salt and pepper.

Pour the egg mixture over the chanterelles in the pan and let set over medium heat. Sprinkle the cheese over it when the egg has set but the surface is still a little damp.

Place the pan in the oven preheated to 175 ° C and cook for about 15 minutes until the cheese has melted.

GREEK FARMER'S PAN

Servings: 4

INGREDIENTS

- 2 Portionen
- 2 tomatoes
- 1 bell pepper
- 1 red onion
- 1 tbsp oil
- 2 tbsp tomato paste
- salt
- pepper
- oregano
- 4 eggs

- 1 pack (s) of feta
- rustic wheat bread

PREPARATION

Wash tomatoes and peppers. Cut into small cubes together with the onion.

Heat the pan, add the oil and sauté the onions. Add the paprika, toss for a few minutes. Finally add the tomatoes and the tomato paste. Season with salt, pepper and oregano. Stir briefly and pour into a bowl.

Put the pan back on the flame. Place four eggs close together in the pan. Let the fried eggs set slightly. Spread the vegetables over the eggs.

Break the feta into two parts, crumble it with your hand over the pan, one part fine, one part coarse. Cover the pan, let the cheese melt.

Scatter some more oregano over the eggs and serve in the pan. A piece of rustic bread goes well with it.

SALTY LASSI WITH MINT

Servings: 4

INGREDIENTS

- 1 cup
- 200 g yogurt
- 100 ml of water
- Pinch (s) of cumin
- Pinch of salt
- 3 mint leaves
- Ice cubes

PREPARATION

Mix the water and yogurt in a blender. Add salt and cumin.

Slightly chop the mint leaves. Fill a glass with ice cubes, add mint and fill up with the lassi. Serve immediately.

CREAMY CHICKEN, ZUCCHINI AND MINT NOODLES

Servings: 4

INGREDIENTS

- 400 g ribbon noodles
- 300 g zucchini
- 1 onion
- 1 clove (s) of garlic
- 1 bunch of mint
- 1 lemon
- 250 g chicken breast fillet
- 1 tbsp rapeseed oil
- 150 g Dr. Oetker crème légère
- salt

- pepper

PREPARATION

Prepare the pasta according to the instructions on the packet.

Wash the zucchini and cut into thin strips with a peeler. Peel onion and garlic and chop finely. Wash the mint, shake dry and finely chop. Squeeze lemon.

Pat the chicken fillet dry and cut into small pieces.

Heat 1 tablespoon of oil, fry the meat and onion. Add the garlic with a little pasta water

Adding more pasta water if necessary. Add most of the mint and season with salt, pepper and lemon juice. Serve with the pasta and sprinkle with the remaining mint.

BEEF STRIPS WITH ZUCCHINI FRIES AND GNOCCHI

Servings: 2

INGREDIENTS

- 400 g tender beef (steak, hip or topside)
- 2 tbsp coconut oil
- 2 shallots
- 100 ml of Pernod
- 300 ml REWE Best Choice unsweetened coconut milk
- 10 g of grainy mustard
- 2 zucchini
- 50 g grated parmesan cheese
- 80 g cashew nuts
- 0.5 hot peppers

- 0.5 clove (s) of garlic
- 70 g polenta (corn grits)
- 1 bunch of flat-leaf parsley
- 1 egg white
- 1 liter of oil for deep-frying
- 150 g gnocchi
- Sea-salt
- Pepper

PREPARATION

Cut the beef into strips. Massage in a tablespoon of coconut oil. Heat a coated pan and fry the meat in it, turning as little as possible. Remove the seared meat from the pan and set aside.

70 g shallots 1 tbsp coconut oil 100 ml of Pernod 300 ml REWE Best Choice unsweetened coconut milk 10 g of grainy mustard

In the same pan, fry 70 g of very finely chopped shallots in a tablespoon of coconut oil until golden brown and sprinkle with Pernod

Let the alcohol boil off completely and add the coconut milk. Reduce again. When the sauce is nice and creamy, stir in the mustard.

For the breading, finely grind grated Parmesan (it is drier than freshly grated Parmesan), cashews, peppers, garlic, corn grits and half of the parsley in a blender and place in a bowl. The consistency should be like breadcrumbs.

Beat the egg whites with the whisk, roll the zucchini strips in them and then turn them loosely in the breading. Heat the oil in a deep saucepan and crisp the fries

Drain the fries on kitchen paper. Wash the rest of the parsley, pat dry well and chop very roughly. Then fry briefly.

Meanwhile, cook and drain the gnocchi according to the instructions on the packet.

Bring the sauce to the boil again, season with salt and pepper, remove from the stove and add the meat.

Arrange the gnocchi, strips of meat and chips on plates and garnish with the fried parsley.

BURRITO WITH CHICKEN

Servings: 4

INGREDIENTS

- 100 g rice
- 350 g chicken breast fillets
- 1 egg
- 0.5 tsp paprika powder
- salt
- pepper
- 250 ml buttermilk
- 100 g corn flakes (unsweetened)
- 50 grams of flour
- 4 tbsp rapeseed oil

- 1 lettuce heart
- 2 large tomatoes
- 4 tortilla wraps
- 2 EL Salad Mayonnaise

PREPARATION

Cook rice according to package directions.

350 g chicken breast fillets 1 egg 0.5 tsp paprika powder salt pepper 250 ml buttermilk 100 g corn flakes (unsweetened) 50 grams of flour 4 tbsp rapeseed oil

Dab the chicken breast fillets. Open the egg in a deep plate, whisk with paprika, salt, pepper and buttermilk. Roughly chop the cornflakes and place them in another deep plate. Roll the pieces of meat in flour, then pull them through the egg mixture and bread them with the cornflakes. Heat the oil in a non-stick pan and fry the meat until golden brown.

Wash the lettuce and cut into individual leaves. Wash and dice tomatoes as well. Heat wraps in a pan without oil for about 20 seconds on both sides, then brush with mayonnaise and top with tomatoes, lettuce, rice and meat.

BAGS WITH PORK NECK, MASHED POTATOES AND MOLE

Servings: 6

INGREDIENTS

- 500 g potatoes
- 100 g carrots
- 3 toe (s) of garlic
- 1 piece of ginger (approx. 2 cm long)
- 150 g butter
- 4 tbsp coconut milk
- 1 bunch of flat-leaf parsley
- 1 bunch of coriander
- 3 spring onions

- salt
- pepper
- 1 can (s) of kidney beans
- 3 teaspoons of water
- 1 teaspoon maple syrup
- 0.5 tsp cocoa
- Chilli powder
- 1 kg pork neck steak
- Sea salt (coarse)
- 8 pancakes

PREPARATION

For the mashed potatoes, peel and roughly chop the potatoes, carrots, garlic and ginger and let them cook together until the potatoes are done. Mash everything into small pieces and mix with the butter and coconut milk. Wash the parsley, coriander and spring onions, chop them up and mix with the mash. Season to taste with salt and pepper.

For the mole, drain the beans and heat them in a saucepan. Add the water, maple syrup and cocoa. Coarsely mash the beans with a fork and season the resulting mixture with salt, pepper and chilli to taste. Preheat the grill.

Season the steaks only with the coarse sea salt and grill them directly on the wire rack. When they have reached the desired core temperature, cut into cubes (approx. 1x1 cm).

Serve the whole dish on a pancake. First a few tablespoons of the mashed potatoes, then some mole and finally the pork neck cubes.

FILLET STEAKS À LA WELLINGTON WITH STUFFED MUSHROOMS

Servings: 4

INGREDIENTS

- 10 mushrooms (large)
- 3 shallots
- 5 tbsp rapeseed oil
- 10 g parsley
- 2 tbsp breadcrumbs
- salt
- pepper
- 1 pack (s) of puff pastry (fresh, refrigerated shelf)
- 4 beef fillet steaks (approx. 180 g each)

- 1 egg yolk
- 2 tbsp whipped cream (lactose-free if necessary)
- 30 g Gouda
- 400 ml beef stock
- 4 tbsp balsamic vinegar
- 1 tbsp cornstarch
- Italian herbs (dried)

PREPARATION

10 mushrooms (large) 3 shallots 3 tbsp rapeseed oil 10 g parsley 2 tbsp breadcrumbs salt pepper

Clean the mushrooms. Remove the stems from 4 mushrooms. Finely chop the remaining mushrooms and stems. Peel and finely dice shallots. Heat 3 tablespoons of oil in a pan, fry the shallots and mushroom cubes. Wash the parsley and finely chop the leaves. Mix the parsley and breadcrumbs with the mushroom mixture, season with salt and pepper.

Take the puff pastry out of the refrigerator. Heat 2 tablespoons of oil in a pan. Season the fillets with salt and fry vigorously on each side for approx. 2 minutes. Cut the puff pastry into 4 squares. Place 2 tablespoons of the mushroom mixture in the center of each square. Put the fillet on top and add 2 tablespoons of the mushroom mixture.

Fill the 4 mushroom hats with the remaining mushroom mixture. Grate the cheese and sprinkle it on the mushrooms. Add the mushrooms to the meat about 15 minutes before the end of the cooking time. Heat the pan in which the meat was fried and sprinkle it with beef stock and vinegar

Boil everything up. Mix the starch with 3 tablespoons of water and add it to the stock tie and let it boil briefly. Season the sauce with the Italian herbs, salt and pepper. Serve the meat with the mushrooms and drizzle with the sauce. Broccoli tastes good with it.

STUFFED KOHLRABI WITH NEW POTATOES AND SPINACH LEAVES

Servings: 4

INGREDIENTS

- 4 kohlrabi
- salt
- 500 g spinach leaves
- 3 toe (s) of garlic
- 2 tbsp olive oil
- 3 slice (s) of bread, e.g. brown bread
- 150 g feta
- 50 g walnut kernels
- pepper

- nutmeg
- 500 g new potatoes
- 250 ml of cream
- 100 ml white wine

PREPARATION

Peel the kohlrabi and cook in the whole tubers in salted water for about 30-35 minutes. Cut off a lid and carefully scoop out the tubers with a spoon or ball cutter. Finely dice the inside.

Clean and wash the spinach. Peel garlic and chop finely. Sweat a third each of the spinach, garlic and all of the kohlrabi cubes in a little oil until the spinach collapses.

Cut the bread and feta into cubes. Chop walnuts. Add everything to the vegetables, season with salt, pepper and nutmeg and pour into the kohlrabi. Place in a baking dish and bake in a preheated oven at 200 ° C top and bottom heat for about 25 minutes.

In the meantime, peel the potatoes, cut into wedges and cook until soft. Briefly blanch the remaining spinach. Heat some oil and sauté the potatoes, remaining garlic and spinach. Add the cream and white wine, reduce a little. Season to taste with salt and pepper. Serve with the filled kohlrabi.

COLORFUL BREAD SALAD WITH TURKEY STRIPS

Servings: 2

INGREDIENTS

- 200 g baguette (gluten-free if necessary)
- 300 g turkey schnitzel
- 100 g mixed salad
- 3 tomatoes
- 1 red onion
- 6 tbsp red wine vinegar
- 12 tbsp olive oil
- 4 teaspoons of honey
- pepper
- salt

PREPARATION

Cut the baguette into slices and dice. Wash turkey escalope, pat dry and cut into strips. Wash the lettuce and spin dry. Wash and chop tomatoes. Peel the onion, cut in half and cut into strips.

For the dressing, mix red wine vinegar, 6 tablespoons of olive oil and honey and season with salt and pepper. Heat 4 tablespoons of olive oil in a pan and toast the bread cubes until golden brown.

Season the turkey strips with salt and pepper and fry them in the remaining olive oil in the pan until golden brown. Mix the tomatoes with the bread cubes, lettuce, onion and dressing in a bowl. Serve with the turkey strips.

CAULIFLOWER RICE PAN WITH MINCE

Servings: 4

INGREDIENTS

- 1 head of cauliflower
- 1 can (s) of kidney beans
- 1 can (s) of corn
- 1 pod (s) of red pepper
- 0.25 bunch of parsley
- 1 onion
- 2 tbsp oil
- 400 g mixed minced meat
- salt
- pepper

- 1 tbsp mustard
- 1 tbsp tomato paste
- smoked paprika powder
- 1 can (s) of chopped tomatoes

PREPARATION

Clean and wash the cauliflower and cut into florets. Shred the florets in the universal chopper to about the size of a grain of rice.

Drain and rinse kidney beans. Drain the corn. Clean and wash the peppers and cut into cubes. Wash the parsley, shake dry and chop. Peel and dice the onion.

Heat the oil in a pan, fry the mince in it until crumbly. Add the onion and bell pepper and fry. Season with salt, pepper, paprika and mustard. Add tomato paste and fry briefly. Deglaze everything with tomatoes, add a little more water if necessary. Add the beans and corn and let everything simmer for about 5 minutes.

Meanwhile, fry the cauliflower rice in two portions without fat in a fragrant pan.

Serve the rice and mincing pan garnished with parsley.

WHOLE WHEAT BURGER

Servings: 4

INGREDIENTS

- 1 yellow pepper
- 4 tomatoes
- 100 g cucumber
- 4 lettuce leaves
- 3 slice (s) of REWE best choice toast bread
- 1 onion
- 400 g ground beef
- 1 egg
- 1 teaspoon mustard
- salt

- pepper
- 2 tbsp oil
- 4 whole wheat rolls
- 4 tbsp tomato ketchup
- 4 slice (s) REWE Best Choice Gouda young 48%

PREPARATION

Halve the peppers, clean, wash, core and cut crosswise into strips. Wash, clean and slice tomatoes. Wash the cucumber and cut into slices. Wash the lettuce and shake dry.

Soak bread. Peel and dice the onion. Knead the mince, squeezed bread, egg, mustard and onion. Season with salt and pepper. Form 4 flat burger patties from the minced meat. Heat oil in a pan. Fry the burger for 5–8 minutes, turning. Remove.

Halve the bun. Brush the lower halves of the bun with ketchup and cover each with a leaf of lettuce. Top with the burger, cheese, bell pepper, tomatoes and cucumber. Put the top halves of the bun on top.

PEA FUSILLI WITH WALNUT PESTO AND RADICCHIO

Servings: 4

INGREDIENTS

- 120 g REWE best choice aromatic walnuts
- 0.5 bunch of parsley
- 1 clove (s) of garlic
- 50 g REWE Feine Welt Parmigiano Reggiano
- 1 tbsp lemon juice
- 1 teaspoon lemon peel
- 50 ml REWE organic extra virgin olive oil
- 400 g REWE Bio Fusilli Green Peas
- salt
- 0.5 head of radicchio

PREPARATION

Wash the parsley, shake dry and pluck the leaves off. Put some leaves aside. Peel the garlic. Grate the parmesan. Put the ingredients in the blender along with lemon juice, lemon zest and olive oil and process into pesto.

Cook the pasta in boiling salted water according to the instructions on the packet.

Cut the radicchio into fine strips, wash and spin dry.

Heat the pasta with pesto in a large saucepan and mix. Briefly fold in the radicchio and mix.

Arrange the pasta in deep plates and garnish with a little fresh parsley.

TAGLIATELLE WITH RADICCHIO AND ROASTED HAZELNUTS

Servings: 4

INGREDIENTS

- 1 head of radicchio
- 50 g hazelnuts
- 10 sprig (s) of thyme
- 12 sage leaves
- 500 g tagliatelle
- salt
- 2 EL Rama Culinesse
- 3 EL Cashewmus
- pepper

PREPARATION

Clean and wash the radicchio, remove the leaves from the stalk and cut into fine strips. Roughly chop the hazelnuts. Wash the thyme, pat dry and pluck the leaves. You Wash the sage and pat dry.

Cook the tagliatelle in salted water according to the instructions on the packet. Collect 1 cup of pasta water.

Gently heat the Rama Culinesse in a pan. Half of the radicchio with half of the thyme and sage in it for 1 minute

Add cashew butter and a little pasta water and heat briefly until a creamy sauce is formed. Season with salt and pepper.

Add the pasta to the steamed radicchio and carefully fold in the fresh radicchio. Serve sprinkled with hazelnuts and the remaining thyme.

ASIAN CAULIFLOWER RICE

Servings: 4

INGREDIENTS

- 2 heads of cauliflower
- 500 g mushrooms
- 2 red peppers
- 2 yellow peppers
- 2 carrots
- 2 spring onions
- 1 piece of ginger
- 1 red onion
- turmeric
- 2 tbsp soy sauce
- 4 tbsp peanut butter
- cumin
- Juice of 0.5 lemon

- salt

PREPARATION

Clean and wash the cauliflower and either chop it in the mixer with the "Pulse" function or grate it finely on the kitchen grater. Clean the mushrooms and cut into thin slices. Clean and wash the peppers and cut into fine strips. Peel the carrots and cut into thin sticks. Clean and wash the spring onions and cut into thin rings. Mix all ingredients in a large bowl.

For the sauce, peel the ginger and grate it finely. Peel and chop the onion. Mix ginger, onion, some turmeric, soy sauce, peanut butter, some cumin and lemon juice in a blender with about 150 ml of water to a creamy sauce. Season to taste with salt. Stir the sauce into the cauliflower mixture.

Wash the coriander, shake dry and roughly chop. Mix the coriander into the cauliflower rice.

MEATBALLS ON SPAGHETTI

Servings: 4

INGREDIENTS

- 2 onions
- 2 toe (s) of garlic
- 3 tbsp olive oil
- 1 can (s) of chopped tomatoes
- salt
- pepper
- sugar
- 200 g carrots
- 400 g ground beef
- 1 egg
- 4 tbsp breadcrumbs
- 300 g whole wheat spaghetti
- 2 zucchini

- 5 stalk (s) of basil

PREPARATION

Peel and finely dice onions and garlic. Heat 1 tablespoon of oil in a saucepan, sauté half of the onion and about 2/3 of the garlic. Deglaze with tomatoes, season with salt, pepper and sugar and simmer covered on low heat.

Peel the carrots and grate finely. Heat 1 tablespoon of oil in a pan, fry the carrots, remaining onion and garlic in it. Take out and let cool down a bit.

Mix the mince, egg, breadcrumbs and carrot mixture together. Season with salt and pepper and shape into small balls.

Prepare the pasta in boiling salted water according to the instructions on the packet. Clean and wash the zucchini and use a spiral cutter to cut into vegetable spaghetti.

Heat 1 tablespoon of oil in a coated pan. Fry the meatballs all around for about 5 minutes. Then take it out and let it steep in the simmering tomato sauce for another 5 minutes.

Add zucchini noodles to the spaghetti boiling water at the last minute. Drain everything and serve the pasta with the meatball sauce. Garnish with basil leaves.

DUCK WITH MANGO AND ORANGE SAUCE AND FRAGRANT RICE

Servings: 4

INGREDIENTS

- 800 g duck breast, ready to cook
- 250 g REWE organic basmati rice
- 2 spring onions
- 20 g ginger
- 1 carrot
- 1 red pepper
- 2 oranges
- 1 ripe mango
- 2 tbsp peanut oil
- 200 ml REWE Feine Welt orange juice
- 0.5 tbsp REWE organic multi-flower honey

PREPARATION

Score the duck breast on the skin side several times with a sharp knife. Place skin side down in a cold pan and fry without fat over medium heat for about 10 minutes. Turn the duck breast and fry for another 5 minutes. Cover the meat and set it aside.

Prepare the rice according to the instructions on the packet. Clean and wash the spring onions and cut into strips. Peel the ginger and carrot and cut into thin slices with the paprika. Peel the oranges and use a knife to remove the fillets from the white layers between them. Peel the mango, cut the pulp from the stone. Cut the pulp into 1 cm cubes. Heat the peanut oil in a pan, fry the spring onions, ginger, paprika and carrots for approx. 3 minutes. Add orange juice, orange fillets, honey and mango and heat for about 1 minute so that the mango and fillets do not disintegrate.

Cut the duck breast into slices and reheat in the sauce. Finally season with salt and pepper and serve immediately.

POKÉ BOWL WITH SALMON

Servings: 4

INGREDIENTS

- 300 g whole grain rice
- salt
- 4 handfuls of spinach leaves
- 0.5 lime
- 2 tbsp sesame oil
- 3 tbsp soy sauce
- 1 tbsp sesame seeds
- 0.5 cucumber
- 2 small avocados
- 1 mango
- 1 small red chilli pepper
- 2 spring onions
- 4 tbsp peanut butter

- Agave syrup
- 4 pieces of salmon fillets
- pepper

PREPARATION

Cook the rice in salted water according to the instructions on the packet.

Wash the spinach and shake dry. Squeeze out the lime juice and mix with 1 tablespoon of oil and 1 tablespoon of soy sauce. Put it on the salad and sprinkle with sesame seeds.

Wash the cucumber and cut into slices. Remove the peel and stone of the avocado pulp and cut into wedges. Remove the mango pulp from the skin and stone and dice. Wash and core the chilli, cut into very fine rings and mix with the mango. Clean and wash the spring onions and cut into fine rolls.

For the dressing, stir peanut butter with 2 tbsp soy sauce until smooth. Season to taste with a little agave syrup.

Heat 1 tablespoon of oil in a non-stick pan and fry the salmon fillets on both sides. Season with salt and pepper.

Arrange rice, salmon, spinach, cucumber, avocado and mango in a bowl. Drizzle with the dressing and sprinkle with spring onions.

RUMP STEAKS WITH ANCHOVY BUTTER

Servings: 4

INGREDIENTS

- 4 REWE organic beef rump steaks (200 g each)
- 1 onion
- 250 g REWE organic sweet cream butter
- 30 ml of cognac
- 6 anchovy fillets
- 30 g capers (glass)
- 1 REWE organic lemon
- herbs of Provence
- salt
- pepper
- 800 g waxy potatoes
- 2 l deep-frying and frying oil
- 4 tbsp olive oil

- Italian herbal salt
- Cayenne pepper
- Sweet paprika

PREPARATION

Take the meat out of the refrigerator. Peel, halve and finely dice the onion. Heat 1 tbsp butter in a small saucepan. Sauté the onions in it. Deglaze with cognac and simmer for 2-3 minutes.

Finely chop the anchovy fillets and capers. Wash the lemon with hot water, rub dry and rub the peel. Beat the rest of the butter with the whisk of the hand mixer until creamy white. Add anchovies, capers, lemon zest and onions. Season with herbs from Provence, salt and pepper. Put butter on cling film, roll up and close the ends of the film. Refrigerate.

Peel and wash the potatoes, cut into sticks and pat dry with a clean tea towel. Heat the frying fat to 140 ° C in a large saucepan. Pre-fry the potato sticks in portions for approx. 4 minutes. Lift out, drain on kitchen paper. Put the pan with the fat aside.

Brush the steaks all around with 1 tablespoon of oil. Heat the grill pan. Fry the steaks on both sides for 3–4 minutes. Remove. Season the steaks with herb salt and cayenne pepper. Wrap the steaks in aluminum foil and leave to rest.

Heat the frying fat again to 175 ° C. Fry the French fries in portions for 4–6 minutes. Lift out, drain on kitchen paper. Season with salt and paprika powder.

Take the steaks out of the foil and arrange on plates. Remove the anchovy butter from the foil, cut into slices and spread on the steaks. Serve with French fries.

TAGLIATELLE NESTS WITH GOAT CHEESE & ROSEMARY

Servings: 4

INGREDIENTS

- 1 clove (s) of garlic
- 100 g REWE Beste Wahl sliced goat cheese
- 250 g REWE Best Choice Cherry Tomatoes
- 1 sprig (s) of fresh rosemary
- salt
- 600 g REWE Best Choice Tagliatelle
- 4 tbsp REWE best choice virgin olive oil
- black pepper (freshly ground)

PREPARATION

Put on a large saucepan with water and bring to a boil.

In the meantime, peel and halve the garlic, dice the goat cheese, wash and halve the tomatoes, wash the rosemary and gently shake dry.

Salt the pasta water, cook the tagliatelle in it until al dente, then drain.

Heat the olive oil in a large pan with a high rim, fry the garlic in it, add the sprig of rosemary and let the oil flavor for a moment. Then remove the garlic and rosemary. Put the tomato halves in the pan, fry briefly.

Put the tagliatelle in the pan and fry with the tomatoes. Sprinkle with the goat cheese and mix, season with salt and pepper. Arrange on plates in nests and serve immediately.

CREAMY CHICKEN, ZUCCHINI AND MINT NOODLES

Servings: 4

INGREDIENTS

- 400 g ribbon noodles
- 300 g zucchini
- 1 onion
- 1 clove (s) of garlic
- 1 bunch of mint
- 1 lemon
- 250 g chicken breast fillet
- 1 tbsp rapeseed oil
- 150 g Dr. Oetker crème légère
- salt
- pepper

PREPARATION

Prepare the pasta according to the instructions on the packet.

300 g zucchini 1 onion 1 clove (s) of garlic 1 bunch of mint 1 lemon

Wash the zucchini and cut into thin strips with a peeler. Peel onion and garlic and chop finely. Wash the mint, shake dry and finely chop. Squeeze lemon.

Pat the chicken fillet dry and cut into small pieces.

Heat 1 tablespoon of oil, fry the meat and onion. Add the garlic with a little pasta water

Stir in the crème légère and add the zucchini strips, adding more pasta water if necessary. Add most of the mint and season with salt, pepper and lemon juice. Serve with the pasta and sprinkle with the remaining mint.

CEVICHE MADE FROM PIKEPERCH, STRAWBERRY & AVOCADO

Servings: 4

INGREDIENTS

- 2 limes
- 2 lemons
- 1 red chilli pepper
- 1 tbsp olive oil
- sea-salt
- 500 g pikeperch
- 300 g strawberries
- 1 teaspoon of liquid honey
- 1 avocado
- 4 stalk (s) of coriander

PREPARATION

Squeeze the limes and lemons. Clean, wash and finely chop the chilli pepper. Beat the citrus juices with olive oil and stir in the chilli and sea salt.

Wash the fish and cut into small cubes, mix with the marinade and leave to stand in the fridge for about 15 minutes, covered.

Clean and wash the strawberries and cut into small cubes, mix with the honey. Halve, core and dice the avocado. Wash the coriander and chop the leaves.

Mix all ingredients and divide into small bowls.

BURRITO WITH CHICKEN

Servings: 4

INGREDIENTS

- 100 g rice
- 350 g chicken breast fillets
- 1 egg
- 0.5 tsp paprika powder
- salt
- pepper
- 250 ml buttermilk
- 100 g corn flakes (unsweetened)
- 50 grams of flour
- 4 tbsp rapeseed oil
- 1 lettuce heart
- 2 large tomatoes
- 4 tortilla wraps

PREPARATION

Cook rice according to package directions.

Dab the chicken breast fillets. Open the egg in a deep plate, whisk with paprika, salt, pepper and buttermilk. Roughly chop the cornflakes and place them in another deep plate. Roll the pieces of meat in flour, then pull them through the egg mixture and bread them with the cornflakes. Heat the oil in a non-stick pan and fry the meat until golden brown.

Wash the lettuce and cut into individual leaves. Wash and dice tomatoes as well. Heat wraps in a pan without oil for about 20 seconds on both sides, then brush with mayonnaise and top with tomatoes, lettuce, rice and meat.

BAGS WITH PORK NECK, MASHED POTATOES AND MOLE

Servings: 6

INGREDIENTS

- 500 g potatoes
- 100 g carrots
- 3 toe (s) of garlic
- 1 piece of ginger (approx. 2 cm long)
- 150 g butter
- 4 tbsp coconut milk
- 1 bunch of flat-leaf parsley
- 1 bunch of coriander

- 3 spring onions
- salt
- pepper
- 1 can (s) of kidney beans
- 3 teaspoons of water
- 1 teaspoon maple syrup
- 0.5 tsp cocoa
- Chilli powder
- 1 kg pork neck steak
- Sea salt (coarse)
- 8 pancakes

PREPARATION

500 g potatoes 100 g carrots 3 toe (s) of garlic 1 piece of ginger (approx. 2 cm long) 150 g butter 4 tbsp coconut milk 1 bunch of flat-leaf parsley 1 bunch of coriander 3 spring onions salt pepper

For the mashed potatoes, peel and roughly chop the potatoes, carrots, garlic and ginger and let them cook together until the potatoes are done. Mash everything into small pieces and mix with the butter and coconut milk. Wash the parsley, coriander and spring onions, chop them up and mix with the mash. Season to taste with salt and pepper.

1 can (s) of kidney beans 3 teaspoons of water 1 teaspoon maple syrup 0.5 tsp cocoa salt pepper Chilli powder

For the mole, drain the beans and heat them in a saucepan. Add the water, maple syrup and cocoa. Coarsely mash the beans with a fork and season the resulting mixture with salt, pepper and chilli to taste. Preheat the grill.

Season the steaks only with the coarse sea salt and grill them directly on the wire rack. When they have reached the desired core temperature, cut into cubes (approx. 1x1 cm).

Serve the whole dish on a pancake. First a few tablespoons of the mashed potatoes, then some mole and finally the pork neck cubes.

FILLET STEAKS À LA WELLINGTON WITH STUFFED MUSHROOMS

Servings: 4

INGREDIENTS

- 10 mushrooms (large)
- 3 shallots
- 5 tbsp rapeseed oil
- 10 g parsley
- 2 tbsp breadcrumbs
- salt
- pepper
- 1 pack (s) of puff pastry (fresh, refrigerated shelf)
- 4 beef fillet steaks (approx. 180 g each)
- 1 egg yolk
- 2 tbsp whipped cream (lactose-free if necessary)

- 30 g Gouda
- 400 ml beef stock
- 4 tbsp balsamic vinegar
- 1 tbsp cornstarch
- Italian herbs (dried)

PREPARATION

Clean the mushrooms. Remove the stems from 4 mushrooms. Finely chop the remaining mushrooms and stems. Peel and finely dice shallots. Heat 3 tablespoons of oil in a pan, fry the shallots and mushroom cubes. Wash the parsley and finely

Chop the leaves. Mix the parsley and breadcrumbs with the mushroom mixture, season with salt and pepper.

Take the puff pastry out of the refrigerator. Heat 2 tablespoons of oil in a pan. Season the fillets with salt and fry vigorously on each side for approx. 2 minutes. Cut the puff pastry into 4 squares. Place 2 tablespoons of the mushroom mixture in the center of each square. Put the fillet on top and add 2 tablespoons of the mushroom mixture.

Fill the 4 mushroom hats with the remaining mushroom mixture. Grate the cheese and sprinkle it on the mushrooms. Add the mushrooms to the meat about 15 minutes before the end of the cooking time. Heat the pan in which the meat was fried and sprinkle it with beef stock and vinegar

Boil everything up. Mix the starch with 3 tablespoons of water and add it to the stock tie and let it boil briefly. Season the sauce with the Italian herbs, salt and pepper. Serve the meat with the mushrooms and drizzle with the sauce. Broccoli tastes good with it.

STUFFED KOHLRABI WITH NEW POTATOES AND SPINACH LEAVES

Servings: 4

INGREDIENTS

- 4 kohlrabi
- salt
- 500 g spinach leaves
- 3 toe (s) of garlic
- 2 tbsp olive oil
- 3 slice (s) of bread, e.g. brown bread
- 150 g feta
- 50 g walnut kernels
- pepper
- nutmeg
- 500 g new potatoes

- 250 ml of cream
- 100 ml white wine

PREPARATION

Peel the kohlrabi and cook in the whole tubers in salted water for about 30-35 minutes. Cut off a lid and carefully scoop out the tubers with a spoon or ball cutter. Finely dice the inside.

Clean and wash the spinach. Peel garlic and chop finely. Sweat a third each of the spinach, garlic and all of the kohlrabi cubes in a little oil until the spinach collapses.

3 slice (s) of bread, e.g. brown bread 150 g feta 50 g walnut kernels salt pepper nutmeg

Cut the bread and feta into cubes. Chop walnuts. Add everything to the vegetables, season with salt, pepper and nutmeg and pour into the kohlrabi. Place in a baking dish and bake in a preheated oven at 200 ° C top and bottom heat for about 25 minutes.

500 g new potatoes 1 tbsp olive oil 250 ml of cream 100 ml white wine salt pepper

In the meantime, peel the potatoes, cut into wedges and cook until soft. Briefly blanch the remaining spinach. Heat some oil and sauté the potatoes, remaining garlic and spinach. Add the cream and white wine, reduce a little. Season to taste with salt and pepper. Serve with the filled kohlrabi.

COLORFUL BREAD SALAD WITH TURKEY STRIPS

Servings: 4

INGREDIENTS

- 2 servings
- 200 g baguette (gluten-free if necessary)
- 300 g turkey schnitzel
- 100mg mixed salad
- 3 tomatoes
- 1 red onion
- 6 tbsp red wine vinegar
- 12 tbsp olive oil
- 4 teaspoons of honey
- pepper
- salt

PREPARATION

Cut the baguette into slices and dice. Wash turkey escalope, pat dry and cut into strips. Wash the lettuce and spin dry. Wash and chop tomatoes. Peel the onion, cut in half and cut into strips.

For the dressing, mix red wine vinegar, 6 tablespoons of olive oil and honey and season with salt and pepper. Heat 4 tablespoons of olive oil in a pan and toast the bread cubes until golden brown.

Season the turkey strips with salt and pepper and fry them in the remaining olive oil in the pan until golden brown. Mix the tomatoes with the bread cubes, lettuce, onion and dressing in a bowl. Serve with the turkey strips.

CAULIFLOWER RICE FRITTERS

Servings: 4

INGREDIENTS

- 1 head of cauliflower
- 2 eggs
- 4 tbsp breadcrumbs
- 100 g grated Gouda cheese
- 2 tbsp hazelnuts
- 5 stalk (s) of parsley
- salt
- pepper
- 0.5 bunch of chives
- 0.5 lemon
- 400 g of grainy cream cheese
- 1 tbsp medium hot mustard
- 1 tbsp olive oil

- 4 tbsp oil

PREPARATION

Clean and wash the cauliflower and cut into florets. Shred the cauliflower florets very finely in the universal chopper and roast them in a coated pan without fat for about 5 minutes while stirring.

Mix the cauliflower rice with the eggs, breadcrumbs and Gouda cheese. Chop the hazelnuts, wash the parsley, shake dry and chop finely. Fold both into the cauliflower mixture. Season with salt and pepper.

Wash the chives, shake dry and cut into fine rings. Squeeze lemon juice. Mix the cream cheese with the chives, mustard and olive oil. Season with salt, pepper and lemon juice.

Shape cauliflower mixture into about 4 cm thick talers. Place on a baking sheet lined with baking paper and brush with oil. Bake in a preheated oven at 180 ° C top / bottom heat for 25 minutes until golden brown. Turn once after 15 minutes.

Serve the cauliflower rice fritters with the dip.

CAULIFLOWER RICE PAN WITH MINCE

Servings: 4

INGREDIENTS

- 1 head of cauliflower
- 1 can (s) of kidney beans
- 1 can (s) of corn
- 1 pod (s) of red pepper
- 0.25 bunch of parsley
- 1 onion
- 2 tbsp oil
- 400 g mixed minced meat
- salt
- pepper
- 1 tbsp mustard
- 1 tbsp tomato paste
- smoked paprika powder

PREPARATION

Clean and wash the cauliflower and cut into florets. Shred the florets in the universal chopper to about the size of a grain of rice.

Drain and rinse kidney beans. Drain the corn. Clean and wash the peppers and cut into cubes. Wash the parsley, shake dry and chop. Peel and dice the onion.

Heat the oil in a pan, fry the mince in it until crumbly. Add the onion and bell pepper and fry. Season with salt, pepper, paprika and mustard. Add tomato paste and fry briefly. Deglaze everything with tomatoes, add a little more water if necessary. Add the beans and corn and let everything simmer for about 5 minutes.

Meanwhile, fry the cauliflower rice in two portions without fat in a fragrant pan.

Serve the rice and mincing pan garnished with parsley.

WHOLE WHEAT BURGER

Servings: 4

INGREDIENTS

- 1 yellow pepper
- 4 tomatoes
- 100 g cucumber
- 4 lettuce leaves
- 3 slice (s) of REWE best choice toast bread
- 1 onion
- 400 g ground beef
- 1 egg
- 1 teaspoon mustard
- salt
- pepper
- 2 tbsp oil
- 4 whole wheat rolls

- 4 tbsp tomato ketchup

PREPARATION

Halve the peppers, clean, wash, core and cut crosswise into strips. Wash, clean and slice tomatoes. Wash the cucumber and cut into slices. Wash the lettuce and shake dry.

Soak bread. Peel and dice the onion. Knead the mince, squeezed bread, egg, mustard and onion. Season with salt and pepper. Form 4 flat burger patties from the minced meat. Heat oil in a pan. Fry the burger for 5–8 minutes, turning.

4 whole wheat rolls 4 tbsp tomato ketchup 4 slice (s) REWE Best Choice Gouda young 48%

Halve the bun. Brush the lower halves of the bun with ketchup and cover each with a leaf of lettuce. Top with the burger, cheese, bell pepper, tomatoes and cucumber. Put the top halves of the bun on top.

PEA FUSILLI WITH WALNUT PESTO AND RADICCHIO

Servings: 4

INGREDIENTS

- 120 g REWE best choice aromatic walnuts
- 0.5 bunch of parsley
- 1 clove (s) of garlic
- 50 g REWE Feine Welt Parmigiano Reggiano
- 1 tbsp lemon juice
- 1 teaspoon lemon peel
- 50 ml REWE organic extra virgin olive oil
- 400 g REWE Bio Fusilli Green Peas
- salt
- 0.5 head of radicchio

PREPARATION

120 g REWE best choice aromatic walnuts 0.5 bunch of parsley 1 clove (s) of garlic 50 g REWE Feine Welt Parmigiano Reggiano 1 tbsp lemon juice 1 teaspoon lemon peel 50 ml REWE organic extra virgin olive oil

Walnuts in a pan without fat

Wash the parsley, shake dry and pluck the leaves off. Put some leaves aside. Peel the garlic. Grate the parmesan. Put the ingredients in the blender along with lemon juice, lemon zest and olive oil and process into pesto.

Cook the pasta in boiling salted water according to the instructions on the packet.

Cut the radicchio into fine strips, wash and spin dry.

Heat the pasta with pesto in a large saucepan and mix. Briefly fold in the radicchio and mix.

Arrange the pasta in deep plates and garnish with a little fresh parsley.

TAGLIATELLE WITH RADICCHIO AND ROASTED HAZELNUTS

Servings: 4

INGREDIENTS

- 1 head of radicchio
- 50 g hazelnuts
- 10 sprig (s) of thyme
- 12 sage leaves
- 500 g tagliatelle
- salt
- 2 EL Rama Culinesse
- 3 EL Cashewmus
- pepper

PREPARATION

Clean and wash the radicchio, remove the leaves from the stalk and cut into fine strips. Roughly chop the hazelnuts. Wash the thyme, pat dry and pluck the leaves. Wash the sage and pat dry.

Cook the tagliatelle in salted water according to the instructions on the packet. Collect 1 cup of pasta water.

Gently heat the Rama Culinesse in a pan. Half of the radicchio with half of the thyme and sage in it for 1 minute

Add cashew butter and a little pasta water and heat briefly until a creamy sauce is formed. Season with salt and pepper.

Add the pasta to the steamed radicchio and carefully fold in the fresh radicchio. Serve sprinkled with hazelnuts and the remaining thyme.

ASIAN CAULIFLOWER RICE

Servings: 4

INGREDIENTS

- 2 heads of cauliflower
- 500 g mushrooms
- 2 red peppers
- 2 yellow peppers
- 2 carrots
- 2 spring onions
- 1 piece of ginger
- 1 red onion
- turmeric
- 2 tbsp soy sauce
- 4 tbsp peanut butter
- cumin
- Juice of 0.5 lemon

- salt

PREPARATION

Clean and wash the cauliflower and either chop it in the mixer with the "Pulse" function or grate it finely on the kitchen grater. Clean the mushrooms and cut into thin slices. Clean and wash the peppers and cut into fine strips. Peel the carrots and cut into thin sticks. Clean and wash the spring onions and cut into thin rings. Mix all ingredients in a large bowl.

For the sauce, peel the ginger and grate it finely. Peel and chop the onion. Mix ginger, onion, some turmeric, soy sauce, peanut butter, some cumin and lemon juice in a blender with about 150 ml of water to a creamy sauce. Season to taste with salt. Stir the sauce into the cauliflower mixture.

Wash the coriander, shake dry and roughly chop. Mix the coriander into the cauliflower rice.

DUCK WITH MANGO AND ORANGE SAUCE AND FRAGRANT RICE

Servings: 4

INGREDIENTS

- 800 g duck breast, ready to cook
- 250 g REWE organic basmati rice
- 2 spring onions
- 20 g ginger
- 1 carrot
- 1 red pepper
- 2 oranges
- 1 ripe mango
- 2 tbsp peanut oil
- 200 ml REWE Feine Welt orange juice
- 0.5 tbsp REWE organic multi-flower honey

PREPARATION

Score the duck breast on the skin side several times with a sharp knife. Place skin side down in a cold pan and fry without fat over medium heat for about 10 minutes. Turn the duck breast and fry for another 5 minutes. Cover the meat and set it aside.

Prepare the rice according to the instructions on the packet. Clean and wash the spring onions and cut into strips. Peel the ginger and carrot and cut into thin slices with the paprika. Peel the oranges and use a knife to remove the fillets from the white layers between them. Peel the mango, cut the pulp from the stone. Cut the pulp into 1 cm cubes. Heat the peanut oil in a pan, fry the spring onions, ginger, paprika and carrots for approx. 3 minutes. Add orange juice, orange fillets, honey and mango and heat for about 1 minute so that the mango and fillets do not disintegrate.

Cut the duck breast into slices and reheat in the sauce. Finally season with salt and pepper and serve immediately.

MEATBALLS ON SPAGHETTI

Servings: 4

INGREDIENTS

- 2 onions
- 2 toe (s) of garlic
- 3 tbsp olive oil
- 1 can (s) of chopped tomatoes
- salt
- pepper
- sugar
- 200 g carrots
- 400 g ground beef
- 1 egg
- 4 tbsp breadcrumbs
- 300 g whole wheat spaghetti
- 2 zucchini

- 5 stalk (s) of basil

PREPARATION

Peel and finely dice onions and garlic. Heat 1 tablespoon of oil in a saucepan, sauté half of the onion and about 2/3 of the garlic. Deglaze with tomatoes, season with salt, pepper and sugar and simmer covered on low heat.

Peel the carrots and grate finely. Heat 1 tablespoon of oil in a pan, fry the carrots, remaining onion and garlic in it. Take out and let cool down a bit.

Mix the mince, egg, breadcrumbs and carrot mixture together. Season with salt and pepper and shape into small balls.

Prepare the pasta in boiling salted water according to the instructions on the packet. Clean and wash the zucchini and use a spiral cutter to cut into vegetable spaghetti.

Heat 1 tablespoon of oil in a coated pan. Fry the meatballs all around for about 5 minutes. Then take it out and let it steep in the simmering tomato sauce for another 5 minutes.

Add zucchini noodles to the spaghetti boiling water at the last minute. Drain everything and serve the pasta with the meatball sauce. Garnish with basil leaves.

RUMP STEAKS WITH ANCHOVY BUTTER

Servings: 4

INGREDIENTS

- 4 REWE organic beef rump steaks (200 g each)
- 1 onion
- 250 g REWE organic sweet cream butter
- 30 ml of cognac
- 6 anchovy fillets
- 30 g capers (glass)
- 1 REWE organic lemon
- herbs of Provence
- salt
- pepper
- 800 g waxy potatoes
- 2 l deep-frying and frying oil
- 4 tbsp olive oil

* Italian herbal salt
* Cayenne pepper
* Sweet paprika

PREPARATION

4 REWE organic beef rump steaks (200 g each) 1 onion 1 tbsp REWE Bio sweet cream butter 30 ml of cognac

Take the meat out of the refrigerator. Peel, halve and finely dice the onion. Heat 1 tbsp butter in a small saucepan. Sauté the onions in it. Deglaze with cognac and simmer for 2-3 minutes.

Finely chop the anchovy fillets and capers. Wash the lemon with hot water, rub dry and rub the peel. Beat the rest of the butter with the whisk of the hand mixer until creamy white. Add anchovies, capers, lemon zest and onions. Season with herbs from Provence, salt and pepper. Put butter on cling film, roll up and close the ends of the film. Refrigerate.

Peel and wash the potatoes, cut into sticks and pat dry with a clean tea towel. Heat the frying fat to 140 ° C in a large saucepan. Pre-fry the potato sticks in portions for approx. 4 minutes. Lift out, drain on kitchen paper. Put the pan with the fat aside.

Brush the steaks all around with 1 tablespoon of oil. Heat the grill pan. Fry the steaks on both sides for 3–4 minutes. Remove. Season the steaks with herb salt and cayenne pepper. Wrap the steaks in aluminum foil and leave to rest.

Heat the frying fat again to 175 ° C. Fry the French fries in portions for 4–6 minutes. Lift out, drain on kitchen paper. Season with salt and paprika powder.

Take the steaks out of the foil and arrange on plates. Remove the anchovy butter from the foil, cut into slices and spread on the steaks. Serve with French fries.